Praise for *Living with Coronavirus*

"S T Kimbrough encompasses themes of compassion and empathy in these nuggets of wisdom and questioning in the form of poetry, and focuses our thoughts on self-growth as well as nurturing others as we navigate the new complexities of a world turned upside down by coronavirus. Grounded in Christian concepts of God's saving grace and our responsibility to our fellow human beings, Kimbrough urges the reader to seek higher ground when we look at our changing world."

—BURTON L. SCOTT, PROFESSOR OF NEUROLOGY;
DIRECTOR, HUNTINGTON'S DISEASE SOCIETY OF AMERICA,
CENTER OF EXCELLENCE AT DUKE UNIVERSITY

"With the graceful simplicity of Wesley hymns, S T Kimbrough's poems bring us face to face with reality—a word that occurs often in this collection. Yet how can anything be face to face in our masked, no-contact Covid-19 world? S T responds to such questions with wry humor, as when he imagines social distancing with the aid of a six-foot selfie-stick. He also can lash out with righteous indignation at the global scope of governmental failure. But in his concluding poems, this man of faith opens before us a horizon of hope. In the face of death, we cannot expect to return to pre-Covid normalcy, but we can 'turn now to love, each one for all.'"

—JOHN H. ERICKSON, FORMER DEAN,
ST. VLADIMIR'S ORTHODOX THEOLOGICAL SEMINARY

"S T Kimbrough is the epitome of what John Ciardi may have had in mind when he wrote, 'Poetry is itself a religion; it gives meaning to life.' S T's poetic gifts express faith, enlivening 'a no-contact world' with an unseen touch, bringing spiritual truth and gracious hope that will enable us to become the help that will overcome our own and others' suffering."

—WILLIAM B. LAWRENCE, PROFESSOR EMERITUS OF AMERICAN CHURCH HISTORY, PERKINS SCHOOL OF THEOLOGY, SOUTHERN METHODIST UNIVERSITY

Living with Coronavirus

Living with Coronavirus

Poems for Suffering, Grieving, Dying, and Living

S T Kimbrough, Jr.
Foreword by Stanley Hauerwas

RESOURCE *Publications* • Eugene, Oregon

LIVING WITH CORONAVIRUS
Poems for Suffering, Grieving, Dying, and Living

Copyright © 2020 S T Kimbrough, Jr. All rights reserved. Except for brief quotations in critical publications or reviews, no part of this book may be reproduced in any manner without prior written permission from the publisher. Write: Permissions, Wipf and Stock Publishers, 199 W. 8th Ave., Suite 3, Eugene, OR 97401.

Resource Publications
An Imprint of Wipf and Stock Publishers
199 W. 8th Ave., Suite 3
Eugene, OR 97401

www.wipfandstock.com

PAPERBACK ISBN: 978-1-7252-8433-3
HARDCOVER ISBN: 978-1-7252-8434-0
EBOOK ISBN: 978-1-7252-8435-7

12/10/20

Contents

Foreword by Stanley Hauerwas   vii
Introduction   ix
Prologue: Christ Weeps   xiii

Section 1: Changed Life

1. Life Has Changed   3
2. A Lost Son   4
3. Acts of Kindness   6
4. Social Distancing   7
5. Sheltering in Place   8
6. Masks   9
7. Mutual Caring   10
8. A No-Contact World   11

Section 2: Governmental Failure

9. How Can Our Government So Fail?   15
10. A Short Ode to the President   16
11. A Joke!   17
12. Blame Has No Cure   18
13. Economy or Welfare?   19

Section 3: The Coronavirus Weapon

14. The Coronavirus as a Weapon   23
15. Unlivable Gaza   25

16. Beware of Covid-19 scams — 27
17. American Racism and Covid-19 — 28
18. Covid-19 and Native Tribes — 29
19. Would You Infect a Child? — 30

Section 4: An Egalitarian Virus

20. This Virus Has No Preference — 33
21. The Struggle Against Coronavirus — 35
22. Everyone — 36
23. The Threat to All — 37
24. Postponed — 39
25. Coronavirus Way of Life — 40

Section 5: Hope

26. Take Time, Learn from Them — 45
27. Normalcy? — 46
28. Hope — 48
29. To Live and To Endure — 49
30. A Common Humankind — 50
31. Unknown Caring Powers — 51
32. Grief and Hope — 53
33. Where Do We Turn? — 54
34. The Gift of Grace — 56
35. How Shall We Live with Coronavirus? — 58
Epilogue: Christ Weeps — 59

Foreword

The challenge is to avoid clichés. That is particularly the case when confronted by unexpected and dramatic events for which we seem to lack adequate description. The current pandemic certainly seems to present that kind of challenge. That it does so makes this small book of poetry all the more a welcome gift. It must be the case that the years of editing the hymns of Charles Wesley has given S T Kimbrough a gift for knowing the right word that makes it possible for him to avoid the cliché. For if poetry is the intensification of language through saying what needs to be said, Kimbrough has accomplished that work in this small and powerful book about the virus.

It is not without significance that Kimbrough is among those whose age makes them particularly vulnerable to the virus. He also lives in a retirement community that increases that risk. Yet there is nothing in these poems that sounds the horn of false courage. Such a stance would threaten to result in the sentimentality that is the death of words necessary to say what is true. It will be clear to anyone reading these poems that S T is a Christian, but his deep theological convictions serve to express his profound love of his and his neighbor's humanity. Indeed, one of the marks characteristic of many of these poems is the recognition that we discover our humanity in the other.

One of my favorite aspects of the world S T's poems creates is the intensification of the everyday. The frying of eggs for breakfast turns out to matter in the face of the pandemic. As Kimbrough makes clear, there is no escape and we dare not entertain false hopes that the threat of the virus will just go away. But we can go on learning again the skills of the everyday, not the least being the recognition of our dependence on our neighbor

The truth of the matter is that no one really knows what has and no doubt will continue to happen given the fact that we really do not know how to defeat the virus. Something has happened, but it is not easy to say what. S T does not try to say he knows what has happened. He, as well as those for whom he writes, remains out of control. But that is why he has given us this book of words that help us go on in the face of suffering and death. We can go on because the words he uses are filled with humor and strength. So let us, as he suggests, wear our masks as a sign of our love for one another.

STANLEY HAUERWAS
Gilbert T. Rowe Emeritus Professor of Theological Ethics
The Divinity School
Duke University
Durham, NC

Introduction

Humankind has endured many kinds of serious plagues that have caused enormous suffering and death. The Plague of Justinian struck Constantinople, capital of the Byzantine Empire, in 541 CE, killing thirty to fifty million people throughout Europe, Asia, North Africa, and Arabia. Eight hundred years later (1347) the Black Death appeared in Europe, killing 200 million over a period of four years. At this time, the concept of quarantine emerged, whereby sailors were kept aboard their ships for thirty to forty days at certain ports.

The Great Plague of London recurred almost every twenty years between 1348 and 1665. Its last occurrence in 1665 depleted the population of London by twenty percent. In just seven months 100,000 Londoners died.

There were terrible outbreaks of smallpox around the world until a vaccine essentially obliterated it. I remember as a child the fear of polio, especially that it might be contagious among children. In Birmingham, AL, where I lived, there was a hospital, The Crippled Children's Clinic, devoted to the treatment of polio victims. There was an annual championship high-school football game at the end of the season, the proceeds of which went to this hospital. I recall quite well as a young boy the day I was given in a sugar cube the first of two doses of the Salk vaccine for polio.

The outbreak of Ebola in Africa and its possible spread to other regions evoked a global awareness and interest in an effective treatment and a vaccine. Now the coronavirus has caused a worldwide pandemic, resulting in thousands of deaths and many more thousands suffering from the symptoms it precipitates.

INTRODUCTION

All of these major health crises have created the awareness of the need for responses of health care specialists and scientists to help find vaccines and viable treatment solutions that will reduce mortality and effectively treat the diseases.

The human effects of these diseases are quite similar: prolonged illnesses, death, disruption of society, the family, the work force, and the economy. There are the accompanying emotional effects of grief, distressed orphaned children, over-stressed hospital staffs, anxieties over the shortage of health workers, medication, and other medical needs. There are also increased incidents of suicide and numerous other emotional entanglements and physical conditions for which a country, city, village, and family are often not prepared.

At times such as these, language becomes extremely important in how we communicate with one another. How we face the realism and facts of the moment is vital for the health of a person and a nation. One notes especially the importance of the language of political leaders at a time of national and global suffering.

We must ask: Do we tell the truth? Are we compassionate and empathetic? Are we friendly? Do we break out of the mold of routine behavior and help others, as we are able? Do we reach out to the least, the lost, and the last in society? Do we hold high human dignity of all no matter who is well, ill, or dying? In this little book of poems many of these questions are addressed both subtly and openly.

>   Economy or our welfare,
>   of these which should come first?
>   . . .
>   The poor, the hungry, homeless folk;
>   they're human just like you.
>   What leader this week of them spoke?
>   We must support them too.
>   . . .
>   Will people of each nation, creed
>   learn from this crisis the world need
>   of *mutual caring* constantly,
>   instead of living recklessly?

INTRODUCTION

. . .

In Gaza what is normalcy,
    where health care is a dream,
and government absurdity
    makes suffering extreme?

. . .

Should this then be the normalcy
    for which we now should seek?
Would this be true democracy—
    to help the strong, the weak?

. . .

"Strengthened or weakened," we ask,
"are those who this virus survive?"

. . .

Why is the truth so hard to see?
Its source is stark reality.

    The awareness of the universality of suffering and death can have a positive effect on people locally, nationally, and globally. This universality reminds us there is one humankind. Epidemics and pandemics are inclusive. They touch people of any race, creed, ethnic or national background. Humankind must take a cue from this universality of diseases and learn to be one people caring for one another.

    Suffering and death are an integral part of living. Of course, we do not suffer equally. A child may be born with a physical problem or congenital condition than can result in prolonged suffering. Accidents may result in all sorts of human injury, sometimes lifelong suffering, and death. Others are stricken with devastating illnesses late in life that can be accompanied by agonizing pain. Sometimes human carelessness results in self-induced suffering, both physically and mentally.

    Suffering and death are at the heart of the Christian faith. God lives both with us through his Son Jesus. Suffering and death are our common heritage, and in this common heritage we are all alike. From the cross Jesus "said to his mother, 'Woman, behold, your son!' Then he said to the disciple [John], 'Behold, your mother!' And from that hour the disciple took her to his own home" (John 19:26–27). In hours of suffering we too need to look to the care of others.

S T Kimbrough, Jr.
Research Fellow
Center for Studies in the Wesleyan Tradition
Duke Divinity School
Durham, NC

Prologue: Christ Weeps

The Christ of Covid-19 weeps
    as for Jerusalem of old.
Close to his open heart he keeps
    a world of illness uncontrolled.

Christ weeps for all who now have died
    and left their dearest ones behind:
a child left with no parent-guide
    and all to suffering now resigned.

Christ weeps for every doctor, nurse,
    who substitute for family, friends
with patients growing worse and worse,
    and with fatigue which knows no ends.

Christ weeps for those who do not care
    and throw all caution to the wind,
whose selfishness lives may not spare,
    and life itself they have chagrined.

Christ weeps and bids us with him weep,
    that we with open hearts will care:
all human dignity will reap,
    this treasure of creation share!

Section 1

Changed Life

1. Life Has Changed

With Covid-19 life has changed,
the "normal" now seems quite estranged.
My favorite restaurant is closed;
the customers might be exposed.
My days now have a different plan;
I cook my own eggs in a pan.
A cook I'm not, everyone knows,
but maybe a new talent grows.
We're told each one, "shelter in place."
I'll try to do it with much grace.
My family, friends I'll telephone,
so they will know they're not alone.
I cannot swim, they closed the pool.
At first, I thought this was quite cruel.
But that was just a selfish thought,
and now I'm thinking as I ought.
Protection, safety both come first,
If not, if ill, I must be nursed.
Yes, life has changed, but that's not bad.
Worldwide concern we've never had.
As this pandemic now we face,
concern for all must leave its trace.

2. A Lost Son

A family lost their son today,
    the death ten thousand twenty-one,
so New York tabulations say.
    His name was Charles, an only son.

Just eighteen years was young Charles' life,
    now mainly by a number known.
He'll never marry, have a wife;
    he leaves his parents all alone.

How could he die at this young age,
    a Covid-19 casualty?
It seems a senseless, vile outrage;
    though brutal, it's reality.

How could it be that Charles was sick,
    for he was careful to stay safe?
He acted like no lunatic:
    at six-feet distance did not chafe.

And though Charles did safe rules observe,
    the virus still he did contract.
By no means did he death deserve,
    but this remains the tragic fact:

as careful as we all may be,
    this vicious virus is a threat
and *all* the public must agree
    to function as one safety net.

When just one person breaks the chain
    of social distancing, we all
are threatened with this virus' pain,
    and even death may us befall.

3. Acts of Kindness

A kind act may surpass most fears
    in face of death, disease.
A teenager, who once she hears,
    her help offers with ease:
her neighbor, Joe, who lives alone,
    can't do from his wheelchair
what many others on their own
    can do as daily fare.

She hears he has no family
    and knocks then at his door,
and learns of the calamity,
    he may go out no more.
"Shelter in place" means he can't shop,
    as usually he might do.
Confined he is at home non-stop
    with little dog named "Blue."

Immediately Jane says to him,
    "I'll help you, Mr. Joe.
I walk 'Blue' with my dog named 'Jim,'
    and to the store I'll go.
Just make a list, when I return
    from walking 'Jim' and 'Blue,'
there'll be no need for a concern,
    I'll go and shop for you."

4. Social Distancing

With social distancing in vogue
    wherever we may go,
I'm trying not to play the rogue,
    though others may think so.

My six-foot brand new selfi-stick
    will really be of use,
If I can teach myself the trick
    to never let it loose.

I'll take it with me everywhere
    and keep folks at six feet
I wonder if they'll be aware
    of this each time we meet.

Like lepers, as the Bible tells,
    cried out, "Lepers are here!"
when meeting see that each one yells:
    "Stay back six feet, you hear?"

5. Sheltering in Place

Can one make sheltering in place,
    a place where love will reign?
Can distance that gives each one space
    help one life to sustain?

When sheltering in place, you show
    you love and that you care,
even those that you will never know,
    their lives you too may spare.

A mask, a shield, the gloves, a gown
    express love and concern.
What fools think they are a "put down"
    of rights for which they yearn?

6. Masks

We think of masks at party time,
    there's something fun about disguise.
A pirate, king, angel, or mime,
    the best mask often wins a prize.

But now a mask's a dire affair,
    for it's become a safety sign.
We've seen the masks health workers wear;
    now masks with gowns, shields, gloves combine.

With my mask, I'm protecting you
    from any germs that I might spread.
Perhaps you should wear a mask too,
    then one the other need not dread.

7. Mutual Caring

While sickness, death, grief shape each day,
and Covid-19 has its sway,
the world is struggling to survive
and asks each day, who's still alive?
One hundred thousand sick or dead,
statistics such as these we dread.
We hear the numbers, not the names,
and yet they're Sally, Jane, and James.
They're people with loved ones and friends,
whose life on ICUs depends.
A doctor, nurse, stands closely by;
how well they know they too may die.
And there are caring volunteers,
who strain each hour to hold back tears.
The bedtime prayers of grief and hope
around the globe give strength to cope.
Will people of each nation, creed
learn from this crisis the world need
of *mutual caring,* constantly,
instead of living recklessly?

8. A No-Contact World

We humans have a need to touch,
    we hug, embrace, and kiss.
For life, our friends are like a crutch,
    and we know what we miss.

The no-contact world of the now
    Coronavirus makes,
evokes the question of just how
    new options it awakes.

We've seen the signs "Please do not touch"
    in stores of antique worth.
We wonder, is this not too much
    across the entire earth?

The mask, the gloves, they are a sign
    of dangers that we face.
Health workers tests with these combine
    Covid-19 to trace.

A minister, rabbi, imam
    now speaks to empty space,
while cameras capture the calm
    and stress seen on his/her face.

We make contact through Facebook, Zoom,
    perhaps we touch the screen,
a gesture to dispel the gloom,
    that daily we have seen.

This no-contact world has a plus
    perhaps we do not see:
when touch we can, we'll not discuss;
    to touch we will agree.

Section 2

Governmental Failure

9. How Can Our Government So Fail?

How can our government so fail
    and care for citizens ignore,
respond each day just like a snail
    as Covid-19 cases soar?

While governors, mayors do their best
    to marshal all the help they can,
our president just thumps his chest
    and acts like he's the top G-man.

Our governors by him are told:
    "Go shop for everything you need.
My Cabinet you dare not scold!
    Don't come to me and plead and plead!"

While patients multiply and die,
    the Fed sends billions to Wall Street.
Our government gets a black eye;
    POTUS' response is: tweet, tweet, tweet!

10. A Short Ode to the President

Why is the truth so hard to see?
Its source is stark reality.
But what is real to some's not true;
they're blind to all but their own view.

"If only others took the time
to realize the fact that I'm
the one who sees things as they are."
And yet his views give truth a jar.

11. A Joke!

Our president oft science ignores;
conceited he just roars and roars:
"Covid-19 is a big joke!"
I said, "My friend just had a stroke!
He coughed so much his veins gave out."
But Trump says, "There can be no doubt,
his cough I'm sure was just a fake.
And if he dies, wow what a break!
Of natural causes your friend died;
his death is not to virus tied.
So Covid-19 deaths are low,
because, my friends, I have said so!"

12. Blame Has No Cure

In dealing with Covid-19,
    the purpose cannot be to blame
the source, and all involved demean
    and cast on them enduring shame.

The source to science matters, sure;
    this may assist with its research
or even help to find a cure,
    but not some people to besmirch.

Whate'er the source, we all must seek,
    whatever we ourselves can do,
to hinder illness of the weak,
    and of the strong prevent it too.

The blame-game is a vile disgrace,
    as politicians seek to save
themselves and thereby truth efface.
    The blame-game will them all deprave.

Think not of blame but help to heal;
    for threatening death, blame has no cure.
Compassion, empathy make real;
    beyond all blame these long endure.

13. Economy or Welfare?

Economy or our welfare,
    of these which should come first?
With Covid-19 do we dare
    to choose and then be cursed?

If people cannot be healthy,
    there is no one to work.
And though you may be quite wealthy,
    you can't even hire a clerk.

Choose corporations or folks' health?
    Must we between them choose?
A government must use its wealth
    for health or it will lose!

A healthy, well-cared-for work force,
    a nation will make strong.
Economy without this source
    cannot, will not last long.

A first priority should be
    the doctors', nurses' care,
that they their patients' needs foresee;
    the public make aware.

The first priority is health
for our economy.
You cannot legislate by stealth
and have a victory.

Section 3

The Coronavirus Weapon

"*Now that we know that the deadly coronavirus can be transmitted through saliva droplets, Israeli soldiers and illegal Jewish settlers are working extra hard to spit at as many Palestinians, their cars, doorknobs, and so on, as possible.*"[1]

14. The Coronavirus as a Weapon

"Hey, spit on Palestinians!"
    Israeli settlers cry.
"We're tired of their opinions,
    with luck, someone may die."

Coronavirus spore by spore
    they could spread with disdain.
The Nazis spat on Jews before
    they put them on a train.

This act relives the holocaust,
    and now Jews act the part
of Nazis who at any cost
    thought prejudice was smart.

---

1. Ramzy Baroud, "The Virus of Occupation: Israelis Have Taken to Spitting on Palestinians During Coronavirus." *MPN News*, April 16, 2020. Baroud reports that the action of spitting on Palestinians and their properties is done by Israeli soldiers and occupying settlers. Thus, spitting becomes the latest tool of racism to subjugate and harm Palestinians. Such acts are criminal in thought and action, yet they go unpunished.

This makes of Coronavirus
 a weapon of attack.
Attackers say, "Spit, inspire us!
 Come on, you'll get the knack."

Is this the way the chosen folk
 display the God they serve?
Or is such service just a joke;
 for God's love, there's no nerve?

15. Unlivable Gaza

In 2010 the UN said,
by 2020 Gaza's dead,
    for no one can live there.
"Unlivable's" the dreadful word
it used, and now it's not absurd;
    a virus it must bear.

Before Coronavirus spread,
with thousands sick and thousands dead,
    the UN did predict:
Gaza would be unlivable,
a matter unforgivable.
    The world is derelict.

An occupying power we blame?
Not only, other lands we name,
    who idly standing by,
care not that children cannot eat
and doctors, sick folk cannot treat.
    Without right care, they die.

Shut down a people who're without;
they can't survive, there is no doubt!
    Is this a humane choice?
Why can't the occupying force
for once now chart a humane course,
    and US leaders, raise their voice?

A humane course means helping those,
ev'n those you think you must oppose,
    no matter their background.
Recall Auschwitz, Stalingrad.
You say that you believe in God:
    help must in you be found.

16. Beware of Covid-19 scams

Beware of Covid-19 scams,
    they multiply each day,
and pharma claims for cures are shams;
    the public lead astray.

The CDC's[2] no proven cure
    in spite of what's been said.
Avoid malaria drugs for sure
    as scientists have pled.

Self-quarantine no one can claim
    assures against disease,
but if you do, you're not to blame
    for Covid's wide reprise.

Calm self-desires, of others think;
    prevent another's death.
This virus you cannot hoodwink,
    lest you breathe your last breath.

---

2. Centers for Disease Control and Prevention.

17. American Racism and Covid-19

Survival is a daily fight
    on most parts of our globe.
Injustice is a daily blight
    which justice ought to probe.
Like Gaza or America,
    in countryside or town,
the poor in Asia, Africa
    are yellow, red, black, brown.

To suffer for one's hue of skin
    is dreadful, without cause.
Despicable is this chagrin
    supported oft by laws.
And now a deadly virus shows
    racism's awful face,
the number of black deaths now grows,
    surpasses any race.

Denied access to good health care,
    access to healthy food,
the poor become our nation's snare,
    while national parties feud.
The vulnerable folk are first
    to suffer from this plague.
This state of things must be reversed.
    Lawmakers, don't be vague!

18. Covid-19 and Native Tribes

Of tribal health care do you think,
    of elders gravely ill,
of little children on the brink:
    high temperatures and chill?

The Native Tribes we oft forget,
    but here were Nations First;
and we can never pay the debt
    with which this land is cursed.

The tribal nation Navajo
    where Covid-19 soars,
now suffers yet another blow,
    not unlike Indian wars.

It's time to think of Navajo,
    of Choctaw, Cherokee.
It's time for good will that we show
    with food, funds, PPE.[3]

The desperate needs of many tribes
    we've often left behind.
It's time the Congress now subscribes,
    more funds for help to find.

---

3. PPE = Personal Protective Equipment

19. Would You Infect a Child?

Would freely you infect a child
with tender skin, demeanor mild?
How easily this can be done
by those whose carelessness can stun.
They keep no distance, wear no mask,
and neither's a demanding task!
A law was made seat belts to wear;
exempting no one, none to spare.
The object, people to protect
and rarely does someone object.
To save another now you're asked,
"Why be a threat and go unmasked?

Section 4

An Egalitarian Virus

20. This Virus Has No Preference

For many Covid-19 means
    they're staying home alone.
For others there are family scenes,
    where routine is—postpone:
postpone daily activities
    like school and bowling frames,
as parents have proclivities
    to learn digital games.

For those who willingly find room
    for challenges online
may see their family on Zoom,
    a talent they'll refine.
Perhaps they'll want the app, WhatsApp,
    to phone a friend in Rome.
There are no costs; it's not a trap;
    they'll do this all from home.

For those who cannot go online,
    and millions are they,
the wealthy must with them align
    and help them save the day.
The US government must give
    support to those in need.
The airlines that breathe not, nor live
    received support with speed.

All those with ingenuity,
    computers, and iPhones
may find they're the minority.
    Life's oft lived by bare bones.
The poor, the hungry, homeless folk;
    they're human just like you.
What leader this week of them spoke?
    We must support them too.

This virus has no preference;
    it claims the young and old
Its global frame of reference
    works like a large blindfold.
There's no vaccine and no known cure;
    one searches in the dark.
Though scientists hope, they can't be sure
    how soon they'll reach the mark.

21. The Struggle Against Coronavirus

It's not a war, it's life or death
    for all who live on planet earth,
preserving humankind's last breath
    and all that is of human worth.

To victors surely go the spoils,
    so reads the history of war.
This is the story it uncoils,
    and what so many wars are for.

To win against a dread disease,
    with no respect for humankind,
will bring no spoils that one may seize
    there's just *new life* that one may find.

Black, yellow, white, bronze, red, and brown,
    new life for all is what is sought.
The right, the left can gain no crown:
    the victory cannot be bought.

For once we must our labels drop,
    join hands with science for new life.
This virus then by chance may stop,
    and unity's a new midwife.

22. Everyone

The deaths of black, brown folk
and elderly astound.
Doctors, nurses face dire threats
without some needs of PPE,[4]
an acronym that we have learned.
Friends and family quarantine
when they test positive.
A patient suffers, dies alone
except for nurses' calming hands.
"Strengthened or weakened," we ask,
"are those who this virus survive?"—
some stronger and some weaker.
Ebola, yellow fever,
and now coronavirus
emphasize mortality,
to which everyone is born.

---

4. PPE = Personal Protective Equipment.

23. The Threat to All

As quietly at home I sit
    with Covid-19 still a threat
I'm solely left to my own wit
    all boring, dull thoughts to forget.

For some there's cabin fever's grip
    on mind and body for a time,
and travel plans for a long trip
    I cancelled; it was not a crime.

Right now, the matter's life or death
    for all who call this planet home.
This threat's no new-born shibboleth,
    far worse than Caesar's fall of Rome.

As long as I am of sound mind,
    my body's kept free of disease,
even though I know I am confined
    I'll gladly use them both with ease.

I'll exercise them both each day;
    perhaps I'll take a walk outside.
I'll phone a friend, respects to pay,
    and read a book I've laid aside.

I'll make a list of things postponed;
    I'll sort through boxes that I stacked
in closets, as if they're disowned.
    Some years have passed since they were packed.

At home in spite of what you think,
    there's plenty left for you to do.
Computers give you an uplink
    to many things that interest you.

Restrictions that may keep you safe
    are: wash your hands, stay six feet back.
At these restrictions do not chafe,
    lest this dread virus you attack.

24. Postponed

"Delayed, cancelled,
nothing available,
everything postponed,"
we hear at every turn.
Covid-19 changes everything!
Now fear and gloom invade
all dimensions of our lives.
We live as on an island, alone
without families for comfort.
A child wonders, "Will I see them?
Will I see mom and dad again?
The word 'corona' makes me sad.
If I can't see them again,
I don't know what I will do.
Someone tell me there is hope."

25. Coronavirus Way of Life

Right now, most things we do say, "Care."
    The mask we wear each day
lets others know we are aware,
    and hence them homage pay.

The shields, the gloves, and the long gowns
    health workers daily wear
let patients know their ups and downs
    these workers risk with care.

Out on the street the people know
    six feet apart means care.
The care for others which they show,
    six months ago was rare.

Coronavirus way of life
    shows us how we should be,
that in the midst of direst strife
    true humanness to see.

Just as the virus knows no creed,
    no race, no party's view,
we learn to care for human need,
    no matter red or blue.

Coronavirus shows us how,
    how daily we should live:
to care for one another *now*,
    for others, ourselves give.

Section 5

Hope

26. Take Time, Learn from Them

Joy, sorrow come so swiftly now
in ways, we cannot disavow.
As nurses, doctors work long hours,
sometimes they feel they've lost their powers,
but when the patients are brought in,
they're ready to begin again.
This time it's a First Responder;
the nurses help, then they ponder:
we've seen him every day this week
as he's brought in the sick, the weak.
Mask, gown, gloves, shield he always wore,
not thinking illness was in store.
Yet even so he now is ill;
with fever trembles and a chill.
Such sacrifice is daily seen
by those who work this tragic scene.
They ask not what's your faith or creed;
their creed: to help all those in need.
All people, take time, learn from them,
whose life's a selfless diadem.

27. Normalcy?

Questions during a pandemic

We hear so much of normalcy
    to which we shall return.
But if you are a refugee,
    for this you do not yearn.

Your normalcy: Where do I dwell?
    How can I feed my child?
Your normalcy is daily hell;
    you live as though exiled.

In Gaza what is normalcy,
    where health care is a dream,
and government absurdity
    makes suffering extreme?

There is no global normalcy;
    its only in your mind.
There is no "normal policy"
    for all of humankind.

Our nation's founders bore witness
    to truths self-evident:
Life, liberty, and happiness
    for *all* was their intent.

Should this then be the normalcy
    for which we now should seek?
Would this be true democracy—
    to help the strong, the weak?

28. Hope

The flowers that know springtime has come,
    know not the world is ill.
They do not know how tragic, glum
    the scene, for they bloom still.

Some flower gardens soon will show
    the gardener's not there;
no evidence of rake or hoe,
    one sees there's been no care.

And still some multi-colored flowers
    bloom on as hopeful signs,
for nature has amazing powers,
    magnificent designs.

Just out my window in the wood
    I see a crocus peak
through fallen leaves to show it could
    new hope for me bespeak.

29. To Live and To Endure

Most days one finds there's charity
    amid Covid-19.
Be thankful it's no rarity
    and surely not routine.

With thousands ill, as many die,
    we pray no selfish prayers.
One lives, one dies we don't know why.
    What science knows, it shares.

Yet science struggles now to learn
    the virus' source and cure,
while people 'round the world all yearn
    to live and to endure.

30. A Common Humankind

Covid-19 we can't abort
    but *all* can lend a hand.
The ill, the dying need support
    from every creed and land.

But patience is in short supply,
    for "shelter in one place,"
makes restlessness oft amplify;
    emotions some displace.

Live not these days in fear of death
    but live in hope of life,
for though we save each other's breath,
    there will be after-strife.

Survival is a noble goal,
    but nobler yet would be
a common humankind that's whole,
    each other's needs to see.

31. Unknown Caring Powers

Cooperate and isolate,
    by now we know the drill.
And yet somewhere it's desolate,
    and there is virus still.

In isolation thoughts run wild:
    Will I infected be?
Will Covid-19 touch my child?
    If so, to what degree?

This desperate isolation
    would seem without an end.
How can one find consolation,
    when one has lost a friend?

Could her death have been prevented
    with earlier caution, care?
If POTUS had not invented
    delay tactics, a snare?

He sets the tone of safe control,
    and other lives can save.
There's life at stake for every soul,
    but how will *he* behave?

In places with the best control
    the virus still can spread,
and Covid-19 takes its toll,
    and precious souls are dead.

I cannot be a fatalist:
    "Whate'er will be, will be."
Each one can be a catalyst
    to help both you and me.

There is a Wiser Will than ours
    that grants to all free will,
a will with unknown caring powers,
    which goodwill can instill.

There's hope that unknown caring powers
    of all will now be used.
And we'll replace the vanished hours
    of some, and time abused.

32. Grief and Hope

I grieve for thousands who have died,
    for thousands who are suffering still,
for front-line workers who have vied
    for PPE[5] awaited still.

I grieve for those who die alone,
    except for doctors/nurses there,
for dying words, spoken by phone,
    for family members who can't share.

I grieve and struggle hope to find,
    and were it not for faith and friends,
I fear I'd be to grief confined.
    My soul with them will make amends.

---

5. Personal Protective Equipment

33. Where Do We Turn?

With death and illness all around,
we wonder where can hope be found.
When there's no Covid-19 cure,
we know some people can't endure.

They can't endure when illness strikes,
especially where infection spikes.
Statistics, data are a key
to help the scientists to see,

to see where people may safe be
and help our leaders to agree,
to act with conscience for us all,
perhaps with conscience of St. Paul.

He said that faith, hope, love remain,
and yet he further did explain,
that one of these is greater far;
yes, love, yes, love is the lodestar.

For all, the love lodestar can guide;
the love lodestar does not divide.
When bodies fail, love is a balm;
to anger, pain, despair brings calm.

If turning back we cannot do,
where shall we turn, to something new?
Turn now to love, each one for all:
Love all, perhaps recall St. Paul.

34. The Gift of Grace

The gift of grace is daily seen
amid the threat: Covid-19.
A nurse's smile and tender touch,
the love a patient needs so much.
When breath is heavy, labored so,
and one lies there and does not know
if dawn will bring another day
and intubated cannot say
a single word without great stress
and fear and anguish can't suppress,
one must have inner strength to see
beyond the pain and fallacy
that life can go on without pain,
a thought existence can't sustain.

How can we learn this from our youth—
we too shall suffer, a stark truth?
Our birth occurs and so our death,
This is no ill-thought shibboleth!
We need not have anxiety,
but face with bold sobriety
the truth that we've a time on earth
to live and celebrate our birth.
To celebrate our lives well-done,
a sister, brother, parent, son,
we're given each a certain time,
to miss this chance would be a crime.

Live with the thought you do not know
when it shall be your time to go.
Though pain and suffering surely come,
rejoice! To gloom do not succumb!
If this seems trite, then be it so,
what better answer do you know?
No, joy cannot remove the pain,
but it can help you start again.
It cannot wipe out suffering, grief;
of mourning it is not a thief.
Your attitude to life adds more
than you have thought could be in store.
So, what you think helps steer the day;
your thoughts have power, give them sway.

35. How Shall We Live with Coronavirus?

How shall we live with pain and grief,
if science finds no quick relief?
If science says it's here to stay,
then we must live another way.
For those who think quite cavalier,
the virus may strike there, not here,
are simply just the fool of fools
who think they can reject the rules.
The rules for safety make demands
beyond just simply washing hands.
The rules require we sanitize
a home, a business, hence be wise.
And social distancing we'll trust;
it's not an option; it's a must.
If we must live this way a year
or more to stave off virus fear,
so be it, we'll await vaccine
that can defeat Covid-19.

Epilogue: Christ Weeps

The Christ of Covid-19 weeps
    as for Jerusalem of old.
Close to his open heart he keeps
    a world of illness uncontrolled.

Christ weeps for all who now have died
    and left their dearest ones behind:
a child left with no parent-guide
    and all to suffering now resigned.

Christ weeps for every doctor, nurse,
    who substitute for family friends
with patients growing worse and worse,
    and with fatigue which knows no ends.

Christ weeps for those who do not care
    and throw all caution to the wind,
whose selfishness lives may not spare,
    and life itself they have chagrined.

Christ weeps and bids us with him weep,
    that we with open hearts will care:
all human dignity will reap,
    this treasure of creation share!

www.ingramcontent.com/pod-product-compliance
Lightning Source LLC
Chambersburg PA
CBHW071745040426
42446CB00012B/2476